Life Processes

SURVIVAL AND CHANGE

Steve Parker

H www.heinemann.co.uk/library
Visit our website to find out more information about Heinemann Library books.

To order:
☎ Phone 44 (0) 1865 888112
🖹 Send a fax to 44 (0) 1865 314091
🖥 Visit the Heinemann Bookshop at www.heinemann.co.uk/library to browse our catalogue and order online.

First published in Great Britain by Heinemann Library, Halley Court, Jordan Hill, Oxford OX2 8EJ, part of Harcourt Education.
Heinemann is a registered trademark of Harcourt Education Ltd.

© Harcourt Education Ltd 2000, 2006
First published in paperback in 2008

Editorial: Clare Lewis
Design: David Poole and Kamae Design
Picture Research: Melissa Allison
Production: Vicki Fitzgerald

Printed and bound in China by WKT

13 digit ISBN 978 0 431 17450 1 (hardback)
10 09 08 07 06
10 9 8 7 6 5 4 3 2 1

13 digit ISBN 978 0 431 17457 0 (paperback)
12 11 10 09 08
10 9 8 7 6 5 4 3 2 1

British Library Cataloguing in Publication Data
Parker, Steve
Life Processes: Survival and change
  – 2nd edition
576.8
A full catalogue record for this book is available from the British Library.

Acknowledgements
The publishers would like to thank the following for permission to reproduce photographs:
Mary Evans Picture Library: p.**28**; Natural History Museum London: pp.**23**, **26**, M Long p.**23**; NHPA: p.**6**, MI Walker p.**4**, Trevor McDonald p.**5**; AP Barnes p.**7**, Jean-Louis Le Moigne pp.**7**, **16**, Andy Rouse p.**8**, Stephen Krasemann p.**9**, Lady Philippa Scott p.**11**, Daniel Heuclin p.**12**, Daryl Balfour p.**13**, A.N.T. p.**13**, David Woodfall p.**14**, Karl Switak p.**15**, Mirko Stelzner p.**17**, Martin Harvey p.**18**, Stephen Dalton p.**19**, T Kitchin & V Hurst p.**20**, Norbert Wu pp.**21**, **27**, Kevin Schafer p.**22**, Anthony Bannister p.**25**, NA Callow p.**28**; Oxford Scientific Films: Liz & Tony Bomford p.**7**, JAL Cooke p.**11**, Rafi Ben-Shahar p.**15**, Doug Allan p.**24**, Konrad Wothe p.**26**; Planet Earth Pictures: Peter Scoones p.**25**.

Cover photograph of a veiled chameleon reproduced with permission of Getty Images/ Image Bank/David Trood.

The publishers would like to thank Mary Jones for her assistance in the preparation of this book.

Every effort has been made to contact copyright holders of any material reproduced in this book. Any omissions will be rectified in subsequent printings if notice is given to the publishers.

CONTENTS

Any words appearing in the text in bold, **like this**, are explained in the glossary.

THE DISTANT PAST

How do we know about conditions on Earth billions of years ago? Layers of rocks have formed one on top of another over millions of years. Parts of animals and plants are preserved in these rocks as **fossils**. They were buried in sand or mud, which gradually hardened and turned to stone. Usually only the hard parts of living things, which do not rot away very quickly after death, form fossils. They include the teeth, bones, claws, horns, and shells of animals, and the wood, cones, and seeds of plants.

CHANGE AND TIME

Fossils and other clues show that conditions on Earth have always been changing. During some periods it was warm and damp, with vast steamy swamps. Other times were cold and dry with massive windy deserts. During great **ice-ages** the land was frozen and snowy. Then came a hot, wet period with floods and tropical rainforests.

As conditions on Earth changed, living things changed too. They had to cope with the new conditions – or risk dying out. This has led to an incredible variety of animals and plants both in the past and today. There are various ideas about how living things have altered over time, to survive and produce the amazing variety of life. These ideas are explained in this book.

► **Fungi**, like this pin-mould, are always ready to decompose dead matter, so the cycle of nature can continue as it has done for millions of years.

SUITED TO DIFFERENT PLACES

Conditions vary around the Earth today, from mountain peaks to deserts, grasslands, forests, rivers, lakes, seashores, and seas. Each of these different places is called a **habitat**. Different animals and plants are suited, or **adapted**, to the various habitats.

- The yak has a warm coat of very long, thick fur to keep out the cold in its mountain home, the Himalayas of Asia.
- The limpet has a tough shell and clings strongly to seashore rocks, so it is protected against crashing waves.
- The deep ocean is very dark and finding food or mates is difficult. So the lantern fish glows to attract its prey or a partner.

▲ The plaice can change its colour to blend in with the seabed so **predators** are less likely to notice it.

DID YOU KNOW ?

Life may have started more than 3 billion years ago. There are tiny, round objects in certain rocks that could be fossils of the earliest simple, microscopic life-forms, like the **bacteria** of today (see page 22).

VARIETY OF LIFE

How many different types of living thing have you seen today? Perhaps a pet dog or cat. Some flowers in the garden or park. There are also many trees and bushes, and grass and weeds. Also birds, butterflies, bees, and flies, worms in soil, spiders in corners. Of course there are the most familiar living things of all – people. To count all of these types of living thing would take a very, very long time.

SPECIES OF LIVING THINGS

Around the world scientists are identifying and counting every type of living thing. This helps us to study and understand the amazing variety of life on Earth and how living things have changed with time.

A single type of living thing is called a **species**. All members of a species look very similar to each other. Also they can breed or **reproduce** with each other to make more of their kind. But they cannot breed with members of other species. For example, tigers are big cats with striped fur. They are one species of big cat. Lions are similar but have tawny fur. They are another, different species. Leopards have spotted fur and are a third species, and so on.

► There could be more than 100 different species of **plankton** in a single drop of seawater.

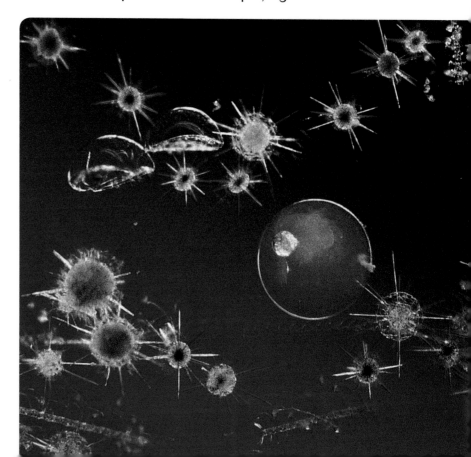

MORE AND MORE SPECIES

Scientists have so far identified and described more than 1.5 million different species. Each species has slight differences from all other species, which make it suited or adapted to survive in its habitat. Scientists have described all kinds of animals and plants, as well as fungi such as toadstools, and microscopic life-forms such as **amoebas** and bacteria. This variety of life is known as **biodiversity**. This variety includes the many different habitats where living things survive, the differences between species, and even genetic differences between individuals in a species.

HOW MANY SPECIES?

No one knows the total number of species on Earth. They have not all been discovered and counted. There could be 10 million, or 15 million, or perhaps more. New species are described almost every week. Most of these are tiny beetles, weevils, and flies from tropical forests, or little worms at the bottom of the sea.

DID YOU KNOW ?

The largest main group of living things in the world is insects. There are well over 1 million species. Within insects, the largest group is the beetles. There are at least 250,000 species of them, probably more. Here are just three beetle species. To show them all would take at least 2,000 books like this one.

▲ Colorado beetle

▲ Cockchafer beetle

▲ Great diving beetle

HOW SPECIES DIFFER

There are many types of bear. There are grizzly bears in North America, brown bears in Europe, Kamchatkan bears from northeast Asia, and Kodiak bears in Alaska. They vary in size and fur colour. But closer scientific study shows that these bears are all very similar. Although they live in different regions in the wild if they are brought together in parks or zoos, they can reproduce with each other. This means they all belong to the same species.

▲ The grizzly is one type of the bear species known as the brown bear.

GEOGRAPHICAL DIFFERENCES

The example of the bears shows that they have differences in their **geography**, which means they live in different places. However, they all eat very similar foods, make dens, and raise cubs in the same way, have similar enemies (chiefly humans), and generally follow very similar lifestyles. This means they have very similar **ecology**.

A RING SPECIES

Herring gulls are one example of a **ring species**. The gulls live in a C-shaped ring around the north of the world, with the two ends in the United Kingdom. In the United Kingdom herring gulls are white, and breed with the herring gulls of eastern United States. The American gulls breed with those of Alaska, and the Alaskan gulls breed with those of Siberia. However, the Alaskan and Siberian gulls get progressively smaller with darker markings the further west you go. At the end of the ring, back in the United Kingdom, the herring gulls have become lesser black-backed gulls, which cannot breed with British herring gulls.

ECOLOGICAL DIFFERENCES

Many types of large animal, such as zebras, antelopes, and gazelles, live in the same place, on the African plains. They have the same geography. They also seem to have the same ecology in that they all eat grass. However, closer study shows differences. Zebras tend to eat the longer grass. Wildebeest (gnu) feed on medium-length grass leaves. Thomson's gazelles graze the shortest grasses. These animals avoid battling for the same food supply by eating grasses of various lengths.

▲ On the African plains, different large grazing mammals, such as zebras and wildebeest, can exist together because they avoid competing for the same food.

BATTLE FOR SURVIVAL

Two species cannot exist with the same geography and ecology at the same time. They would be direct **competitors** and battle for the same needs such as food and shelter. One species would soon adapt better to the conditions and gradually take over, while the other species died away – unless it also changed. This battle for survival is the central reason why living things change with time.

DID YOU KNOW ?

Some species of plants are adapted to growing quickly on bare new land, for example after a fire, earthquake, or volcanic **eruption**. They are called **pioneer species**. They spring up and breed in a short time, spreading seeds far and wide. Gradually, slower-growing plants take over and crowd them out. However, by then the pioneer species have reproduced and moved on to new, fresh ground.

SURVIVAL ON THE EDGE

The best conditions for life are year-round warmth, sunshine, and moisture. This is why tropical rainforests are bursting with an incredible biodiversity of animals and plants. What about places on Earth with the worst conditions for life? These include the freezing Arctic **tundra**, the endless cold blackness of the ocean depths, and deserts where it has not rained for years. Even in such severe and extreme conditions, living things find a way to survive.

LIFE PROCESSES AND BODY CHEMISTRY

Every living thing has thousands of natural chemical substances inside its body. These substances are constantly combining together, splitting apart, and undergoing other changes or reactions. These changes are known as body **metabolism** and are the processes that make up life itself.

A slight difference from normal in one of these chemical substances may affect metabolism by, for example, allowing a chemical change in the body to happen at a higher temperature. A series of such changes can mean that the whole metabolism becomes adapted to working at higher temperatures. When this happens the living thing can survive in warmer places than it lived in before.

IN FREEZING SEAS

Ice-fish live in polar seas where the water temperature is below freezing point, 0°C (32°F). The fish do not turn to ice because they have special natural **anti-freeze** substances in their blood and body fluids. These substances are similar to the anti-freeze chemicals we put into the engines of cars and other vehicles. The chemicals mean that the ice-fish can survive in a habitat that would normally kill other creatures.

IN HOT SULPHUR SPRINGS

Some natural hot springs have water heated deep in the rocks inside the Earth that is so hot it would scald us. However, there are bacterial **microbes**, such as *Thiobacillus thioxidans* that can withstand the temperature. They feed on the sulphur-containing minerals dissolved in the water, which are rich in energy and **nutrients**.

▲ Brine shrimps live in water that is too salty for almost any other living thing.

IN WARM SALTY WATER

The seas contain small amounts of dissolved salt and are home to many living things. Salt-lakes in hot regions have up to 10 times the level of salt found in the sea. Too much salt can be harmful yet brine shrimps are adapted to dwell in salt-lakes and many birds come to feed on them.

▲ An Arabian oryx in Oman

DID YOU KNOW ?

Arabian oryx, a rare type of antelope, live in the baking deserts of the Middle East. In the scorching midday Sun their body temperature can rise by 5°C without harm. This increase would kill most other mammals by heatstroke. The oryx cool down again in the evening.

Unwelcome Guests

A species in its original region and habitat is usually part of the balance of nature. Its numbers are kept in check in numerous ways. These include predators of the species, competitors for food, living space, and nest sites, **parasites** such as fleas and lice, various diseases, and severe climate conditions such as a cold winter. Sometimes animals and plants are taken, accidentally or on purpose, to new places that lack these ecological checks and controls. The new or **introduced species** can upset the balance in its unnatural home, and sometimes breed out of control to become a very serious pest.

SPREADING AROUND THE WORLD

One example of an introduced species is the European or common rabbit. In its original home of southwest Europe and northwest Africa, rabbits are a natural part of the countryside. In other places, such as Australia, they are very numerous and widespread pests. Rabbits began to spread in Australia from about 1900. Now they eat farm crops, compete with local animals for plant food, take the goodness from the soil and reduce it to dust, weaken banks with their burrows, and spread diseases.

Why has the rabbit become such a pest? It is an adaptable animal, able to live in a variety of habitats and eat a range of foods. It breeds very quickly. In Australia it has fewer predators compared to its original home where its numbers are kept down by foxes, wild cats, stoats, and similar hunters.

▲ The prickly pear or opuntia cactus was taken from the United States to Australia as a hedge-type plant. It soon spread to cover immense areas. Local plant-eating animals could not cope with its sharp spines.

FROM PEST CONTROLLER TO PEST

Sugar cane is a valuable crop in north-east Australia. But sugar cane beetles are serious pests and damage the cane fields. In 1935 one of their natural predators, the cane toad, was brought from South America to Australia to keep the beetles in check. However, this big, powerful, and poisonous toad moved from the cane fields into the surrounding bush. It bred quickly and began to eat the local animals, causing some of them to become rare. Cane toads have now become serious pests themselves.

CONTROLLING NUMBERS

Disease is one form of ecological check or control. Red-knee disease has killed many frogs and similar amphibians in recent years. Whether this is a natural outbreak, or caused by a human change such as **pollution**, is not clear.

► The cane toad oozes a poison that may kill an animal, such as a dog, that tries to eat it.

DID YOU KNOW ?

The water hyacinth is probably the world's worst water-weed. Its natural home is the tropical waterways of South America but it has been introduced into Africa and Asia and spread to cover vast areas. Its thick floating masses squeeze out local plants, prevent plants growing in the dark water below, choke rivers and canals, and prevent travel by boats.

◄ Water hyacinths in a National Park in Zimbabwe (Lake Kariba)

PRODUCING OFFSPRING

Species stay separate from other species because, when their members breed or reproduce, they produce young of their own species. A mother lion gives birth, not to baby tigers or leopards, but to baby lions. Seeds from a Scots pine tree grow, not into Corsican pines or Norway pines, but into young Scots pine trees. This seems very obvious but how does it happen? How are the features of a living thing passed on from parents to offspring in order to continue the species?

▲ Scots pines in the Cairngorms, Scotland

INSTRUCTIONS FOR LIFE

Each living thing grows and develops according to a set of instructions called **genes**. These are similar to the plans and instructions for building a complex structure such as a jumbo jet or skyscraper. However, genes are not written on paper! They are in the form of string-like lengths of a chemical known as **DNA** (deoxyribonucleic acid).

BUILT-IN BEHAVIOUR

Offspring inherit many features from their parents – even types of behaviour. For example, ants not only grow up to look like other ants in their nest, they also carry out tasks such as cleaning, collecting food, and defending the nest, without learning or being taught. The ants inherit their behaviour in the form of genes. This is called instinctive (in-built) behaviour.

GENES IN CELLS

The strings of DNA may be quite long but they are incredibly thin. They are coiled up tightly inside the microscopic building blocks or **cells** that make up all living things. Large living things such as rhinos, trees, or humans have billions of cells. Each cell in a human body contains DNA with more than

▲ Baby lions receive or inherit certain behaviour, such as how to lie still if danger is near.

100,000 genes. The lengths of DNA from one human cell added together would stretch almost 2 metres (6.5 feet).

PASSING ON GENES

When a female and male of a species breed, they both pass their genes to their offspring. The offspring grow and develop according to these genes. This is why offspring look similar to their parents. The passing on of features or characteristics from parents to offspring, in the form of genes, is known as **heredity**.

DID YOU KNOW ?

Many living things reproduce when a female and male breed together. This is **sexual reproduction**. Some living things reproduce on their own, without the need for a breeding partner. This is **asexual reproduction**. For example, the creosote bush sends out new stems, which grow their own branches and become new bushes, in a ring around the parent. The offspring came directly from one parent so they all have exactly the same genes. They are called **clones**.

EVERYONE IS DIFFERENT

Have you ever seen a breeding colony of seabirds such as gannets? Thousands of birds flap, wheel, soar, and dive, calling and squawking to their chicks in the close-packed nests. How do they tell each other apart? They all seem the same but look closer and there are small differences. Some gannets are bigger than others. Some have slightly longer beaks or slightly wider wings. In fact the gannets are not all the same. They are varied and in nature even tiny variations are important. Variations could mean the difference between life and death.

▲ Gannets may look the same but they have slight differences and these differences could affect their survival.

SIMILAR BUT NOT THE SAME

Part of the variation between living things is due to their genes. In the above example, all of the gannets are from the same species, so they have similar genes. However, their genes are not exactly the same. There are two reasons for this.

MIXING GENES

First, the genes are not simply passed on as a complete set from parent to offspring. The genes from mother and father are "mixed" during breeding. Each offspring receives its own unique combination or set of genes. It is different from the genes of its mother and father, different from the genes of the other offspring, and different from the genes in every other member of its species. The "mixing" is known as **genetic recombination**.

CHANGING GENES

Second, the DNA that forms the genes must be copied so it can be passed to the offspring. Sometimes the copying is not exact. The gene is changed or altered and the offspring receives the new version. This changed gene may have no effect on the offspring, or it may cause an alteration such as a difference in size, shape, colour, or body chemistry. The change may be helpful or harmful. Such a change in a gene is called a **genetic mutation**.

VARIETY IN THE GARDEN

Beautiful flowers grow and blossom in the garden. Flowers of the same breed or variety are similar but they are not exactly the same. Some differences come from their slightly different genes. Others are due to the different conditions where they live. Flowers growing in the shade of a tree may not be as tall and healthy as flowers growing in full sunshine.

▲ Small variations in conditions, such as drier soil or less sunshine, will affect how flowers grow.

DID YOU KNOW ?

Sometimes living things have exactly the same genes, for example in asexual reproduction (see page 15). Identical twins are another example. They start as one tiny egg which would normally grow into a single living thing. However, the egg divides into two and then each of these halves goes on to develop into a whole living thing.

ONLY SOME SURVIVE

As we have seen on page 9, two species cannot exist with the same geography and ecology at the same time. One species adapts better to the conditions while the other species dies away or changes. This "battle" also occurs within a species.

A WORLD FULL OF BOARS?

Wild boars live in forests across Europe and Asia. The mother wild boar gives birth to up to 10 small, striped boarlets each year. She may do this from when she starts breeding at the age of about four years, until she becomes too old, at perhaps fifteen years. If all wild boar females did this, wild boars would soon cover all the land on Earth. Of course, this does not happen – not all the offspring survive.

▲ Baby wild boar look similar but the slight differences between them can decide if they survive and grow or become a meal for a predator.

THE STRUGGLE FOR LIFE

Baby wild boars have many predators and so their lives are a struggle for survival. Cats such as leopards and tigers stalk them. Wolves and other wild dogs catch them. Eagles and big hawks can carry them away.

It is not simply luck that determines which boarlets survive. They are all different, with slightly different genes (see page 16). One youngster may have a new feature that gives a slight advantage in survival. This could be a different striped coat pattern for better **camouflage** in the undergrowth, or a stronger **instinct** to stay still and quiet when danger is near.

PASSING ON THE ADVANTAGE

The baby boar with the advantage is more likely to survive, grow up, and have offspring of its own. It will pass on its genes, with the new feature, to its offspring. They will also be more likely to survive and breed compared to boars that lack the feature. Gradually, over many generations, over thousands of years, the feature becomes more common among wild boars. Eventually they all have it. Very slightly, the whole species has changed.

CHANGE BY ARTIFICIAL SELECTION

Long ago people captured wild boars and bred together only those that were less fierce, easier to tame, and more likely to produce plenty of meat. Gradually, over thousands of years, this selection by people, known as **artificial selection**, produced modern farm pigs. Other farm animals, from horses and cows to sheep, goats, turkeys, and chickens have all been bred from wild ancestors by artificial selection.

GRADUAL CHANGE

This type of change happens not only in wild boars but in all living things. It is called **evolution**. The species changes or evolves with time, becoming more suited to the conditions as new and better features constantly appear. Change occurs by the process called **natural selection** (see page 21).

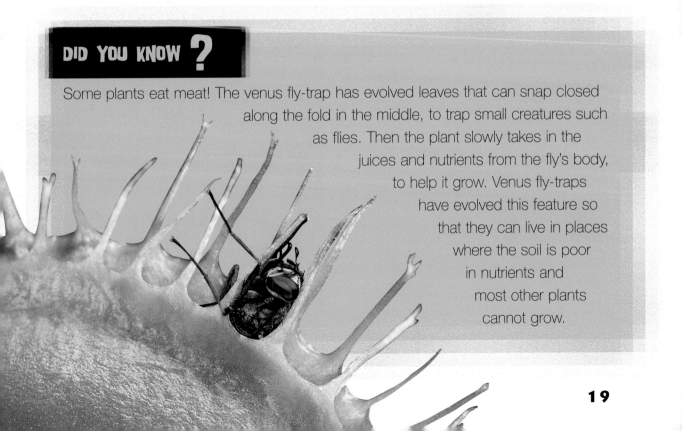

DID YOU KNOW ?

Some plants eat meat! The venus fly-trap has evolved leaves that can snap closed along the fold in the middle, to trap small creatures such as flies. Then the plant slowly takes in the juices and nutrients from the fly's body, to help it grow. Venus fly-traps have evolved this feature so that they can live in places where the soil is poor in nutrients and most other plants cannot grow.

CHANGE INTO NEW SPECIES

Tree shrews are small creatures that look like a combination of shrew and squirrel. However, they are unlike any other mammals and form their own group, called the tupaiids. They live only in the forests of east and south Asia, and eat small animals such as insects and worms as well as some seeds and fruits. There are about 18 species of tree shrews, yet they all look very similar to each other and live similar lifestyles. How did the different species come about?

BECOMING SEPARATE

Imagine one tree shrew species spread across a large forest. During a time of heavy rain, a new river forms and its waters split the forest into two. Then a volcano erupts and forms a mountain barrier, separating the forest into more parts. A huge fire burns and causes another split in the forest. During a storm some trees are swept down the river, carrying a few tree shrews in their branches. They float across a narrow patch of sea to another forest on a nearby island.

NEW SPECIES

The single species of tree shrew has been separated in three or four isolated patches of forest. As time passes, conditions in each patch of forest become slightly different. Gradually, the tree shrews change too, as they adapt by natural selection to suit their own surroundings. They cannot breed with their relatives in the other patches. Slowly they become different from them. The original single species of tree shrew evolves into a number of new species.

▲ Different species of tree shrews look similar as they have probably evolved from one ancestral species.

EVOLUTION AND DIVERSITY

In this way one species may evolve and split into two or more species. The evidence for this process is all around us; it is why similar species of living things, such as the tree shrews, occur in groups or **families** of species. They are similar because they are closely related, having evolved from the same original or ancestor species.

This process of evolution into new species has happened countless times, with all kinds of living things, over millions of years, all over the Earth. It has given rise to the amazing diversity of life both in the past and in the world that we see today.

EVOLVING EELS

Garden eels live in burrows on the seabed. Over long periods of time the sea levels have changed, the water temperature has become colder or warmer, and other conditions have altered. Garden eels in different regions have evolved to suit conditions there, and there are now more than 100 different species.

▲ These garden eels are adapted to the warm waters of the Caribbean.

EVOLUTION BY NATURAL SELECTION

In 1859 English naturalist Charles Darwin (1809–1882), in his book *On the Origin of Species*, suggested how evolution happens. In the struggle for life, some individuals are better suited or adapted than others. These are more likely to survive, breed, and pass the adaptations to their offspring. It seems that nature itself chooses or selects who lives or dies. Darwin called this idea the theory of evolution by natural selection. It is the theory accepted by nearly all scientists today.

PREHISTORIC LIFE

The process of evolution by natural selection explains how living things change or evolve over millions of years. It also explains why there are fossils in the rocks of living things that once thrived but then disappeared. As conditions changed on Earth, new species of plants, animals, and other living things appeared. Some species could not cope and died out or became **extinct**. Others changed or evolved, became better adapted and continued to survive.

EARLY FORMS OF LIFE

Fossils suggest that the earliest forms of life on Earth were single microscopic cells (see page 5). However, life-forms gradually became bigger and more complicated. From about one billion years ago, seaweeds and soft-bodied animals, such as worms and jellyfish, began to appear in the seas. This period of time, between 4,600 and 570 million years ago, is called the Precambrian Era.

ANCIENT LIFE

At the start of the Paleozoic Era, or "Ancient Life" (570–248 million years ago), the first shelled animals evolved. They included trilobites, ammonites, and brachiopods (lampshells). Then the first fish appeared in the seas. By 350 million years ago sharks similar to those of today swam in the oceans. The first small plants grew on land, followed by the first land animals such as millipedes and insects, then amphibians and reptiles.

▲ A trilobite fossil

DID YOU KNOW ?

Trilobites were ancient cousins of crabs and prawns. However, most of their fossils are not of the whole creatures, but of the shells they cast off or moulted.

MIDDLE LIFE

Perhaps the most famous prehistoric animals are dinosaurs. These first walked the land about 230 million years ago, near the start of the Mesozoic Era or "Middle Life" (248–65 million years ago). The earliest mammals, small and shrew-like, appeared about the same time. Winged reptiles called pterosaurs flew in the air, and fish-shaped reptiles such as ichthyosaurs (see page 26) swam through the seas. The first birds such as *Archaeopteryx* also evolved at this time.

▲ The earliest known bird, *Archaeopteryx*, lived about 150 million years ago.

RECENT LIFE

At the end of the Mesozoic Era a great change happened and many kinds of animals and plants disappeared, including dinosaurs, pterosaurs, and ichthyosaurs. This is called a **mass extinction**. The reason for this may be that a giant block of rock, called a meteorite, smashed into the Earth from space. It caused such great and sudden changes that many species could not survive. This marked the beginning of the Cenozoic Era or "Recent Life" (from 65 million years ago to now). Mammals and birds evolved rapidly and became very widespread, as they are today.

▲ *Hyracotherium*

BIGGER AND FASTER

Fossils through the ages show how horses have evolved to become bigger. *Hyracotherium* of 50 million years ago was hardly bigger than a pet rabbit. *Mesohippus* of 30 million years ago was about the size of a large pet dog. The reason for the larger size may have been to run faster and escape from predators – since these were also evolving to become bigger.

THEN AND NOW

Fossils in the rocks show that most animals, plants, and other living things have changed or evolved over time. However, a few kinds have not. As far as we can tell from fossils, these species today are very similar to living things that thrived millions of years ago. Such animals and plants are sometimes called "living fossils". How have they managed to survive almost unchanged over such great periods of time?

GOOD DESIGN FIRST TIME

A species may have survived because evolution produced a living thing that could cope with many conditions, such as different habitats, a range of foods, and a variety of predators. The adaptable design needed little change through time. Sharks are an example. They appeared in the seas more than 300 million years ago and their overall body design is still the same today.

STABLE SURROUNDINGS

Some types of habitat are very stable. They hardly change with time. So there are few new threats or dangers to cause the living thing to evolve. Fossils show that brachiopods, or lampshells, were some of the first ever shelled creatures, appearing in the seas almost 600 million years ago. The mud on the deep ocean floor is much the same now as it was then, and so are the brachiopods.

▲ Brachiopods (lampshells) have changed little in almost 600 million years.

SLOW EVOLUTION

Some living things change quickly and become very specialized for their habitat and conditions. When the conditions change again they are so specialized that they cannot continue to evolve and they die out. However, living things that evolve slowly may be able to cope better with the ever-changing surroundings, by small alterations and adjustments. The velvet worm (*Peripatus*) is a combination of legless worm and many-legged millipede, with the benefits of each design. Similar worms lived more than 550 million years ago.

▼ The velvet worm still survives among the rotting leaves on the tropical forest floor, as it has done for hundreds of millions of years.

DID YOU KNOW ?

Scientists once thought that a fish called the coelacanth died out over 50 million years ago. However, in 1938 a living coelacanth was discovered in the Indian Ocean near the Comoros Islands. Since then several more have been found.

▲ A coelacanth

JUST LUCKY?

Fossils of the ginkgo tree, also called the maidenhair tree, go back more than 100 million years. This tree was thought to be extinct but scientists discovered it growing in China. Ginkgoes have now been planted around the world in parks and gardens. The ginkgo could just be a lucky survivor – a species that evolution forgot.

THE SAME BUT DIFFERENT

Among the ocean waves, a grey back with a curved fin shows briefly above the surface. At a glance it is not possible to identify the animal properly. It could be a shark. It might be a different type of fish such as a marlin or swordfish. It may be a dolphin or a young whale. All of these animals are similar in size and in the shape of their back and fin yet they belong to very different animal groups. Why do they look so similar?

BECOMING THE SAME

Moving through water takes much more effort than moving through air. A smooth, streamlined shape makes swimming easier. Many fast water creatures have a similar body shape, including sharks and other fish, squid, dolphins, porpoises, whales, and even seals and otters. They are long with a pointed front end, a smooth bulge in the middle and a tapering rear end. They have flaps called fins or flippers to help push them through water and control their movements. Such animals are not similar because they are closely related. They have simply evolved similar body shapes to solve the same problem of swimming fast. This is known as **convergent evolution**.

◄ A dolphin has a smooth, streamlined shape to slip quickly through the water.

▼ An ichthyosaur is a type of extinct reptile that lived at the time of the dinosaurs. Its body shape was very similar to that of a dolphin.

BECOMING DIFFERENT

A different type of evolution can also occur. Living things that were close relatives and so had similar body features, can gradually become dissimilar. This happens if they live in different places and have different ways of life.

For instance, the fins of the first fish were probably used for swimming. Evolution has since produced many other uses for fins. The lionfish has fan-like fins with poison spines for defending itself. The gurnards and tripodfish have spiky walking fins. Mudskippers and climbing perch have fleshy, muscular, arm-like fins to pull themselves along on land. The remora has a sucker-shaped fin on its back to stick to a shark or other large creature and hitch a ride through the ocean. This is called **divergent evolution**.

SPINES IN DEFENCE

Desert animals are often desperate for food and water so they nibble at desert plants. Many very different desert plants have evolved the same defence against being eaten – thorns and spines. These plants include cacti, euphorbias, and acacias (thorn trees).

◄ The lionfish's front fins are shaped like sharp spines for jabbing poison at enemies.

◄ The remora's upper fin is shaped like a sucker for clinging to a larger animal such as this shark.

SURVIVAL AND CHANGE TODAY

Until about 10,000 years ago most of the world was unaffected by people. Then humans started to plant crops, keep farm animals, and build villages and towns. The world began to change faster. Now vast areas of once-wild land are used for farming, building, quarrying, mining, roads, parks, and leisure. Humans are changing the world more quickly than ever before. Can animals and plants change to cope?

CHANGING TOO FAST

Extinction is a natural part of evolution and has happened since life began. Today, too many species cannot cope with the increased speed of change. Hundreds have died out already. The rate of extinction has speeded up from around one species every hundred to a thousand years, to one species every day. The process of evolution by natural selection works too slowly for them to adapt to the way humans are changing the planet.

THREATS TO WILDLIFE

Some animals are killed to make decorative fur coats or trophies such as horns and tusks. They include elephants, rhinos, and gorillas. Some are killed for no other reason than "sport". Collection from the wild for the pet and plant trades affects species such as parrots, monkeys, orchids, and cacti. Pollution of the air, soil, and water threatens many other species.

▲ About 1,000 years ago, New Zealand was home to the giant moa, a large flightless bird. Now they have all died out – probably hunted to extinction by people.

HELPING WILDLIFE SURVIVE

By far the largest threat to wildlife is habitat loss. This is when humans destroy natural places and change the land for our own use, such as making farms, golf courses, towns, roads, ports, shopping centres, and factories. Wild animals and plants simply have nowhere left to live.

The best thing people can do to help these threatened species is to slow down, stop, and then reverse the process of habitat loss. People can reduce pollution and the use of rare natural resources such as hardwood trees. Action is needed to conserve the beautiful and fascinating variety of wildlife around the world for people in the future.

▲ Bumblebees have become very rare in some regions because the flowers where they gather their nectar have been sprayed with pesticide chemicals.

DID YOU KNOW ?

Some types of tourism are harmful to wildlife, such as when people collect living corals. However, some tourism can be helpful. People pay to watch rare animals such as gorillas and whales. They do not disturb the animals and the money is used to help local wildlife. This is called eco-tourism.

CAPTIVE BREEDING

Some species are so rare that their only hope may be captive breeding. The animals are brought to wildlife reserves, parks, or zoos where they will hopefully breed. Their offspring are then carefully put back into suitable wild places. This captive breeding has been successful for several species such as golden lion tamarins, Californian condors, Arabian oryx, and Przewalski's horses.

GLOSSARY

adapt, adaptation change in a feature of a living thing that helps it to fit into its surroundings, or environment, and improve its chances of survival

amoeba tiny single-celled organism

anti-freeze chemical substance that does not freeze solid when it becomes very cold

artificial selection when people, rather than the forces of nature, choose which living things survive and breed

asexual reproduction when something reproduces by dividing in two, or when a bud or runner on a plant splits off to produce another individual

bacteria minute living things, only visible under a microscope, and found almost everywhere on Earth

biodiversity range or variety of living things in a habitat

camouflage blending in with the surroundings, usually by shape, colour, and pattern, to be less noticeable

cells single units or "building blocks" of living things. Most cells are tiny, only 1/30th of a millimetre across (far smaller than the dot on this i).

clones identical living things that have exactly the same genes

competitors living things that try to obtain the same substance or requirement, such as food, shelter, or a place to nest

convergent evolution when different living things change or evolve so that they appear to be similar, usually because they have similar lifestyles

divergent evolution when similar living things change or evolve so that they become different, usually because they lead lifestyles that are different from each other

DNA de-oxyribonucleic acid, a chemical substance in living things that carries information in the form of genes

ecology, ecological how animals, plants, and other living things survive together in their surroundings

eruption when a volcano spurts out fumes, ash, and red-hot, molten runny rock or lava

evolution when living things change or alter (evolve) over time

extinct, extinction when every member of a group or species has died, so that the group or species no longer exists

family in nature, a group of similar types or species of living thing. Lions, tigers, leopards, cheetahs, and jaguars form the big cat family.

fossil remains of a once-living thing that have been buried or preserved and turned to stone in rocks

fungi large kingdom (group) of living things that obtain their nutrients and energy by decaying or decomposing other living things. Moulds, mushrooms, and toadstools are fungi.

gene information in the form of a body chemical, DNA, which carries the instructions for a living thing to develop and survive

genetic mutation when genes change due to an alteration in the chemical code of their DNA

genetic recombination when genes are "mixed" and come together in new, different groupings or combinations

geography features of the Earth's surface, such as mountains, seas, and rivers

habitat distinctive type of place or surroundings, such as a woodland, mountain top, grassland, pond, or seashore

heredity process of passing genes and characteristics from parent to offspring

ice-age very cold time in Earth's history, when snow and ice covered much more land and sea than today

instinct, instinctive when an animal has the information about how to carry out an action in its genes, without having to learn

introduced species type of animal or plant that is taken to a new region where it does not naturally occur

mass extinction when many species of living thing die out (become extinct) at about the same time

metabolism changes that occur in the chemicals and other substances inside the body of a living thing

microbe tiny micro-organism that can only be seen under a microscope. Bacteria are microbes.

natural selection when the forces of nature, such as severe weather or lack of food, affect which living things survive and breed

nutrient substance needed by a living thing for its growth, development, and survival

parasite living thing that lives on and feeds off another living thing, called the host, and harms the host in the process

pioneer species one of the first or earliest species in a new or strange place

plankton tiny plants and animals that live in the water of lakes, seas, and oceans

pollution when unnatural and harmful substances collect in a place, harming or interfering with life there

predator living thing that hunts, catches, and kills other living things, its prey, for food

reproduce when a living thing breeds or makes more of its own kind

ring species species that alters gradually across the wide area where it lives, so that in some places its members look different

sexual reproduction reproduction or breeding that requires both a male and a female parent

species group of living things that look similar to each other and can breed together, but that cannot breed with other living things

tundra flat, treeless region in a very cold place, where the soil is frozen solid for part of the year

FIND OUT MORE

Internet research

You can find out more about adaptation on the Internet. Use a search engine such as www.google.com or www.yahooligans.com to search for information. A search for something general such as "animal survival" will bring back lots of results but it may be difficult to find the information you want. Try refining your search to look for some of the specific animals, plants, or ideas mentioned in this book, such as "coelacanth" or "genetic mutation".

More books to read

Chinery, Michael. *Secrets of the rainforest: Predators and prey*. London: Cherrytree books, 2000

Strauss, Rochelle. *Trees of life*. London: A & C Black, 2006

INDEX